PRINCEWILL LAGANG

Respectful Disagreements: A Guide to Healthy Conflicts

First published by PRINCEWILL LAGANG 2023

Copyright © 2023 by Princewill Lagang

All rights reserved. No part of this publication may be reproduced, stored or transmitted in any form or by any means, electronic, mechanical, photocopying, recording, scanning, or otherwise without written permission from the publisher. It is illegal to copy this book, post it to a website, or distribute it by any other means without permission.

Princewill Lagang asserts the moral right to be identified as the author of this work.

First edition

This book was professionally typeset on Reedsy.
Find out more at reedsy.com

Contents

1	Introduction	1
2	Understanding Conflict	4
3	The Role of Respect	7
4	Communication Techniques	10
5	Embracing Different Perspectives	13
6	Managing Emotional Responses	16
7	Identifying Triggers and Patterns	19
8	Finding Common Ground	22
9	Using "I" Statements	25
10	Strategies for De-escalation	28
11	Seeking Solutions Together	31
12	Growing Through Conflict	34

1

Introduction

Welcome to the first chapter of our book, where we embark on a journey to explore the art of navigating conflicts in a respectful and constructive manner. In a world where interactions and relationships are an integral part of our lives, conflicts are almost inevitable. However, what sets successful relationships apart is not the absence of conflicts, but the way we handle them.

1.1 Navigating Conflicts: A Delicate Art

Conflicts are an inherent part of human interaction. Whether it's a disagreement at work, a difference of opinion among friends, or a misunderstanding within a family, conflicts have the potential to either strengthen or weaken relationships. In this book, we will delve deep into the dynamics of conflicts, examining the underlying causes and the various strategies to navigate them effectively.

1.2 The Power of Communication and Conflict Resolution

At the heart of managing conflicts lies the power of effective communication and conflict resolution. Communication is not merely about conveying our thoughts; it's about truly understanding one another. We'll explore how miscommunication often fuels conflicts and how actively listening and expressing ourselves can create an atmosphere of understanding.

Conflict resolution is not just about reaching compromises; it's about finding solutions that honor the needs and feelings of all parties involved. We will discuss the significance of empathy, compromise, and finding common ground while respecting individual differences.

1.3 The Significance of Constructive Conflict

While conflicts are often seen in a negative light, they can also be opportunities for growth and change. Constructive conflicts, when managed well, can lead to innovation, improved relationships, and personal development. We'll examine real-life examples of individuals and groups that have turned conflicts into stepping stones for positive outcomes.

1.4 The Roadmap Ahead

In the upcoming chapters, we will dive deeper into the various aspects of conflict resolution. We will explore techniques for effective communication, strategies to de-escalate tensions, methods to identify and address underlying issues, and the importance of self-awareness in conflict situations. Each chapter will provide practical insights, actionable tips, and relatable scenarios to help you navigate conflicts in your own life.

As we embark on this journey, keep in mind that conflict resolution is not a one-size-fits-all approach. Every situation is unique, and the tools and techniques you'll learn in this book can be tailored to fit various contexts. Remember, the goal is not just to resolve conflicts, but to strengthen relationships and foster a culture of respect, understanding, and growth.

INTRODUCTION

So, let's begin our exploration into the realm of conflict and communication, and discover how we can transform conflicts from stumbling blocks into building blocks for better relationships.

2

Understanding Conflict

In this chapter, we'll delve into the fundamental nature of conflict and its role in relationships. We'll also explore the crucial distinction between healthy disagreements and destructive arguments, as understanding this difference is essential for effective conflict resolution.

2.1 The Nature of Conflict: Inevitable and Complex

Conflict is an integral part of human interaction, stemming from differences in perspectives, values, needs, and desires. It is essential to recognize that conflicts are not inherently negative; rather, they can be opportunities for growth and understanding. As we engage with others, the clash of ideas and interests is natural and can lead to innovative solutions and enhanced relationships.

2.2 The Spectrum of Disagreements: Healthy vs. Destructive

Not all conflicts are created equal. It's important to distinguish between healthy disagreements and destructive arguments. Healthy disagreements are characterized by respectful communication, a focus on the issue at hand,

and a willingness to listen to opposing viewpoints. These conflicts can lead to mutual understanding, improved decision-making, and strengthened relationships.

On the other hand, destructive arguments are marked by hostility, personal attacks, and a lack of constructive communication. These conflicts can escalate quickly, damage relationships, and hinder productive problem-solving. Recognizing the signs of destructive arguments is crucial in order to take steps to prevent them from spiraling out of control.

2.3 The Role of Emotions in Conflict

Emotions play a significant role in conflicts. They can intensify disagreements, cloud rational thinking, and lead to impulsive reactions. Understanding the emotional component of conflicts is essential for effective resolution. Learning to manage and express emotions in a healthy way can help de-escalate tensions and create an environment conducive to productive discussions.

2.4 Exploring Underlying Issues

Beneath the surface of conflicts often lie deeper, underlying issues. These issues can stem from past experiences, unmet needs, or differing values. Exploring and addressing these root causes is essential for resolving conflicts sustainably. By identifying and addressing the underlying issues, we can prevent recurring conflicts and pave the way for more harmonious relationships.

2.5 Developing Conflict Awareness

Developing conflict awareness involves recognizing the signs of impending conflicts, understanding our own triggers, and being attuned to the emotions and cues of others. By cultivating this awareness, we can anticipate conflicts, take proactive steps to manage them, and approach disagreements with a clear and open mindset.

2.6 Embracing Constructive Conflict

Ultimately, conflicts are an opportunity for growth, learning, and strengthening relationships. Embracing constructive conflict means approaching disagreements with an open heart and a willingness to understand the other party's perspective. It involves active listening, empathy, and a commitment to finding solutions that benefit everyone involved.

2.7 Chapter Summary

In this chapter, we explored the nature of conflict, acknowledging its inevitability in relationships. We distinguished between healthy disagreements and destructive arguments, emphasizing the importance of constructive communication. We discussed the role of emotions and underlying issues in conflicts, and the significance of conflict awareness. By embracing constructive conflict, we set the stage for effective resolution and improved relationships.

In the next chapter, we'll delve into the realm of effective communication, a cornerstone of conflict resolution. We'll uncover strategies for expressing ourselves, active listening, and fostering understanding, all of which are vital tools for navigating conflicts successfully.

3

The Role of Respect

In this chapter, we'll delve into the pivotal role that mutual respect plays in the context of disagreements and conflict resolution. We'll examine how respect forms the bedrock for productive and constructive conflict resolution, fostering healthy relationships and meaningful outcomes.

3.1 The Essence of Mutual Respect

At the heart of effective conflict resolution lies the concept of mutual respect. Respect involves valuing the opinions, feelings, and perspectives of others, even when they differ from our own. It's the foundation upon which open communication, empathy, and understanding are built.

3.2 Respect as a Two-Way Street

Respect is not a one-sided endeavor; it's a reciprocal exchange. For conflicts to be resolved successfully, all parties involved must demonstrate respect for one another. This means listening actively, refraining from personal attacks, and acknowledging the validity of differing viewpoints.

3.3 Creating a Safe Environment

Respect creates a safe environment where individuals feel comfortable expressing themselves honestly and without fear of judgment. When people feel respected, they're more likely to share their thoughts openly, leading to deeper understanding and better problem-solving.

3.4 Empathy and Respect

Empathy, the ability to understand and share the feelings of another, goes hand in hand with respect. When we put ourselves in someone else's shoes and genuinely try to see the situation from their perspective, we're practicing respect. Empathy humanizes conflicts, making it easier to find common ground and reach compromises.

3.5 Respecting Boundaries

Respect also involves recognizing and honoring personal boundaries. During conflicts, emotions can run high, and it's crucial to respect each individual's need for space, time, and emotional comfort. This demonstrates a high level of consideration and fosters an environment where conflicts can be approached with a clear mind.

3.6 Transforming Disagreements with Respect

When respect is present, disagreements transform into opportunities for growth. Instead of trying to "win" an argument, the focus shifts to understanding and collaboration. This shift not only leads to more effective conflict resolution but also strengthens the foundation of relationships.

3.7 Navigating Power Dynamics

Respect is especially crucial when power dynamics are at play. In professional settings, personal relationships, or any situation where one party holds more influence, showing respect becomes a means of promoting fairness, equity, and inclusivity.

3.8 Chapter Summary

In this chapter, we explored the essential role of mutual respect in conflicts and conflict resolution. We highlighted how respect creates a conducive environment for open communication, empathy, and understanding. By demonstrating respect for others and their viewpoints, we establish a strong foundation for navigating conflicts constructively.

In the next chapter, we'll dive into the art of effective communication, uncovering techniques for expressing ourselves clearly, actively listening, and fostering understanding in the midst of disagreements.

4

Communication Techniques

In this chapter, we'll explore essential communication strategies that are integral to successful conflict resolution. We'll delve into techniques such as active listening, interpreting non-verbal cues, and expressing ourselves clearly and assertively.

4.1 The Power of Active Listening

Active listening is a cornerstone of effective communication, especially during conflicts. It involves giving your full attention to the speaker, refraining from interrupting, and seeking to understand their perspective without judgment. By truly hearing the other person, you show respect and create an environment conducive to mutual understanding.

4.2 Non-Verbal Communication: Beyond Words

Non-verbal cues such as facial expressions, gestures, and body language often convey more than words alone. In conflict situations, paying attention to these cues can provide insights into the speaker's emotions and intentions. Likewise, being aware of your own non-verbal signals helps ensure that your words align with your message.

4.3 Clear Expression of Thoughts and Feelings

When conflicts arise, expressing yourself clearly is paramount. Clearly articulate your thoughts, feelings, and concerns without resorting to blame or accusations. Use "I" statements to convey your emotions and viewpoints while taking responsibility for your own perspective.

4.4 Using "I" Statements

"I" statements shift the focus from blaming the other person to expressing your own emotions and needs. For example, instead of saying, "You never listen to me," you could say, "I feel unheard when I sense that my opinions are being dismissed." This approach fosters understanding rather than defensiveness.

4.5 Avoiding Defensive Responses

Defensiveness can hinder effective communication. Instead of immediately countering an opposing viewpoint, take a moment to reflect and respond thoughtfully. This prevents escalation and allows for a more productive exchange of ideas.

4.6 Asking Open-Ended Questions

Asking open-ended questions encourages dialogue and invites the other person to share their perspective more fully. These questions typically begin with "what," "how," or "why," prompting thoughtful responses that can lead to deeper understanding.

4.7 Reflective Summarization

Summarizing what the other person has said demonstrates that you're actively engaged and seeking to comprehend their viewpoint. Reflective summarization not only helps clarify your understanding but also shows respect for the other person's input.

4.8 Remaining Calm and Composed

During conflicts, emotions can run high, but maintaining a calm and composed demeanor is crucial. Taking deep breaths and practicing mindfulness can help you stay centered and focused, even in the midst of intense disagreements.

4.9 Chapter Summary

In this chapter, we explored communication techniques that are vital for effective conflict resolution. Active listening, interpreting non-verbal cues, using "I" statements, and remaining calm are all key components of successful communication during conflicts. By mastering these techniques, you can create an atmosphere of understanding and openness, paving the way for productive resolutions.

In the next chapter, we'll take a closer look at the process of de-escalating conflicts and managing emotions, further enhancing your ability to navigate disagreements constructively.

5

Embracing Different Perspectives

In this chapter, we'll delve into the significance of valuing diverse viewpoints during conflicts and how doing so can lead to personal and relational growth. We'll explore techniques for empathetic listening and seeking a deeper understanding of differing perspectives.

5.1 The Richness of Diverse Viewpoints

Diverse viewpoints are like pieces of a puzzle that, when combined, create a fuller picture. In conflicts, different perspectives offer a broader understanding of the situation and potential solutions. Embracing these viewpoints allows for innovative thinking and the opportunity to challenge our own assumptions.

5.2 The Role of Empathetic Listening

Empathetic listening involves putting yourself in the other person's shoes and genuinely seeking to understand their thoughts and emotions. It's a powerful tool for fostering empathy, opening lines of communication, and building bridges between opposing viewpoints.

5.3 Suspending Judgment

Suspending judgment is a crucial step in embracing different perspectives. When you approach a conflicting viewpoint with an open mind, you create an atmosphere that encourages honest expression and reduces defensiveness.

5.4 Seeking Understanding Through Questions

Asking questions to understand the reasoning behind a viewpoint can illuminate the other person's motivations and beliefs. This approach shows respect and a genuine interest in comprehending their perspective.

5.5 Reflective Listening

Reflective listening involves paraphrasing the other person's statements to ensure you've accurately understood their viewpoint. It demonstrates that you're actively engaged and committed to truly comprehending their thoughts.

5.6 Finding Common Ground

Seeking common ground doesn't mean sacrificing your own values, but rather identifying shared interests or goals. This can create a foundation for collaboration and resolution that benefits all parties involved.

5.7 Embracing Cognitive Flexibility

Cognitive flexibility is the ability to adapt your thinking based on new information. During conflicts, this skill allows you to consider alternative viewpoints without feeling threatened, fostering a sense of growth and adaptability.

5.8 Developing Empathy

Empathy is the cornerstone of embracing different perspectives. By cultivating an understanding of another person's emotions and experiences, you can better navigate conflicts with compassion and consideration.

5.9 Chapter Summary

In this chapter, we explored the value of embracing diverse viewpoints during conflicts. Empathetic listening, suspending judgment, seeking understanding, and finding common ground are techniques that promote effective communication and resolution. By fostering cognitive flexibility and empathy, you can navigate conflicts in a way that not only strengthens relationships but also encourages personal and relational growth.

In the next chapter, we'll delve into the process of de-escalating conflicts and managing strong emotions, providing you with tools to navigate challenging situations with grace and poise.

6

Managing Emotional Responses

In this chapter, we'll delve into the critical role that emotions play in conflicts and how they can impact the resolution process. We'll explore techniques for managing emotional reactions, maintaining composure, and fostering an environment conducive to productive conflict resolution.

6.1 The Influence of Emotions on Conflict

Emotions have a profound impact on conflict situations. They can intensify disagreements, cloud rational thinking, and hinder effective communication. Recognizing and managing emotions is key to resolving conflicts constructively.

6.2 The Importance of Emotional Awareness

Emotional awareness involves recognizing and understanding your own emotions as well as those of others. Being attuned to your emotions helps you respond thoughtfully rather than react impulsively during conflicts.

6.3 Taking a Step Back

When emotions run high, taking a step back can provide valuable perspective. Temporarily removing yourself from the situation allows you to cool off, gather your thoughts, and approach the conflict with a clearer mind.

6.4 Practicing Mindfulness

Mindfulness involves being fully present in the moment without judgment. By practicing mindfulness, you can stay grounded during conflicts and prevent emotions from spiraling out of control.

6.5 Emotional Regulation Techniques

Emotional regulation techniques, such as deep breathing, counting to ten, or visualizing a calming scenario, can help you manage intense emotions and prevent them from dictating your responses.

6.6 Reframing Negative Thoughts

Negative thoughts can fuel emotional reactions during conflicts. Reframing these thoughts involves looking at the situation from a different perspective and challenging assumptions, leading to more balanced and rational responses.

6.7 Communicating Emotions Constructively

Expressing emotions is healthy, but it's important to do so constructively. Use "I" statements to convey your feelings without blaming, and avoid using accusatory language that might escalate the conflict.

6.8 Recognizing Escalation Triggers

Understanding your personal triggers that escalate emotions is crucial for managing conflicts effectively. By recognizing these triggers, you can take proactive steps to prevent escalation and maintain composure.

6.9 Creating Time and Space

If emotions become overwhelming, it's okay to request time and space to regroup before continuing the discussion. This allows everyone involved to manage their emotions and return to the conflict with a clearer perspective.

6.10 Chapter Summary

In this chapter, we explored the impact of emotions on conflict resolution and discussed techniques for managing emotional responses. Emotional awareness, mindfulness, and emotional regulation are tools that can help you navigate conflicts with composure and clarity. By mastering these techniques, you can create an environment that promotes rational thinking and productive communication, ultimately leading to more effective conflict resolution.

In the next chapter, we'll delve into the process of finding common ground and generating win-win solutions, enhancing your ability to reach resolutions that satisfy all parties involved.

7

Identifying Triggers and Patterns

In this chapter, we'll explore the importance of identifying common triggers and recurring patterns in conflicts. We'll delve into how self-awareness can play a crucial role in breaking unproductive cycles and fostering more constructive conflict resolution.

7.1 Understanding Triggers and Patterns

Triggers are situations, words, or actions that activate strong emotional reactions. Patterns refer to recurring sequences of behavior or reactions that tend to repeat in conflicts. Recognizing these triggers and patterns is essential for gaining insights into your own behavior and finding effective ways to address conflicts.

7.2 Common Conflict Triggers

Certain situations often trigger emotional responses during conflicts. These triggers can include feeling misunderstood, criticized, dismissed, or unsupported. Understanding your personal triggers allows you to anticipate and manage your emotional reactions.

7.3 Recognizing Recurring Patterns

Recurring patterns in conflicts are behaviors, responses, or dynamics that repeat over time. For example, avoiding conflicts altogether, becoming overly defensive, or resorting to blaming can be common patterns. Recognizing these patterns helps you break free from unproductive cycles.

7.4 The Role of Self-Awareness

Self-awareness involves understanding your thoughts, emotions, and behaviors. By cultivating self-awareness, you can identify your triggers and patterns and make conscious choices to respond differently during conflicts.

7.5 Self-Reflection and Analysis

Regular self-reflection and analysis of past conflicts help you identify what triggered certain reactions and which patterns emerged. This process allows you to gain insights into your own behavior and make adjustments for more positive outcomes in the future.

7.6 Seeking Feedback

Seeking feedback from trusted individuals about your behavior during conflicts can provide valuable perspectives. Others may notice triggers and patterns that you might have missed, helping you gain a more comprehensive understanding of your conflict dynamics.

7.7 Implementing Strategies for Change

Once you've identified triggers and patterns, you can develop strategies to manage them more effectively. These strategies may involve setting boundaries, using relaxation techniques, reframing negative thoughts, or seeking professional guidance.

7.8 Embracing Constructive Change

Breaking unproductive cycles requires a commitment to constructive change. This involves taking ownership of your triggers and patterns, learning from mistakes, and actively working towards more effective conflict resolution.

7.9 Chapter Summary

In this chapter, we explored the significance of identifying triggers and patterns in conflicts. Recognizing common triggers and recurring patterns is crucial for understanding your own behavior and responses. By cultivating self-awareness, engaging in self-reflection, seeking feedback, and implementing strategies for change, you can break unproductive cycles and foster more constructive conflict resolution.

In the final chapter, we'll bring together all the insights and techniques we've explored throughout the book, providing you with a comprehensive approach to navigating conflicts in a respectful and constructive manner.

8

Finding Common Ground

In this final chapter, we'll delve into the art of finding common ground and generating win-win solutions during conflicts. We'll explore why seeking shared goals is essential and provide strategies for effective collaboration and compromise.

8.1 The Value of Common Ground

Finding common ground means identifying areas of agreement and shared goals, even amid differing viewpoints. It's a key component of constructive conflict resolution, as it allows parties to work together toward solutions that benefit everyone involved.

8.2 Fostering Open Dialogue

Open dialogue is the foundation for finding common ground. By encouraging open and respectful communication, you create an environment where all parties can share their perspectives and interests.

8.3 Identifying Shared Goals

Even in the midst of disagreements, there are often shared goals that both parties can agree upon. Identifying these common objectives provides a starting point for collaboration and compromise.

8.4 Brainstorming Solutions

Brainstorming involves generating a range of potential solutions to the conflict. Encourage creativity and explore various options that align with shared goals, even if they require some degree of compromise.

8.5 Seeking Win-Win Solutions

Win-win solutions are those that satisfy the interests and needs of all parties involved. These solutions often involve flexibility, creativity, and a focus on the bigger picture rather than winning the argument.

8.6 The Art of Compromise

Compromise involves giving up some of your own desires in exchange for meeting the needs of others. It's a crucial skill in conflict resolution, demonstrating a willingness to find middle ground.

8.7 Building Bridges, Not Walls

Instead of becoming entrenched in your own viewpoint, strive to build bridges between differing perspectives. This involves looking for commonalities, reframing differences, and finding ways to connect.

8.8 Integrating Different Ideas

Integrative solutions involve combining elements of different proposals to create a solution that satisfies multiple interests. This collaborative approach can lead to innovative and comprehensive outcomes.

8.9 Evaluating Solutions

After generating potential solutions, evaluate each one against the shared goals and interests. Assess the feasibility, potential outcomes, and long-term impact of each solution before reaching a decision.

8.10 Chapter Summary

In this final chapter, we explored the significance of finding common ground during conflicts. Seeking shared goals, fostering open dialogue, brainstorming solutions, and embracing compromise are strategies that promote effective collaboration and win-win outcomes. By focusing on solutions that benefit all parties involved, you can transform conflicts into opportunities for growth, understanding, and strengthened relationships.

As you apply the insights and techniques from this book, remember that conflict resolution is a continuous journey of learning and improvement. By navigating conflicts with respect, effective communication, empathy, and a commitment to finding common ground, you can foster a culture of constructive conflict resolution in all areas of your life.

9

Using "I" Statements

In this chapter, we'll dive into the powerful technique of using "I" statements for effective communication during conflicts. We'll explore how "I" statements help express feelings and needs without assigning blame, ultimately fostering an environment of open dialogue and understanding.

9.1 The Power of "I" Statements

"I" statements are a communication tool that allows you to express your feelings, thoughts, and needs without coming across as accusatory or confrontational. They promote respectful communication and encourage the listener to empathize with your perspective.

9.2 Expressing Emotions Clearly

"I" statements involve clearly articulating your emotions without assuming negative intentions on the part of the other person. For instance, instead of saying, "You never listen to me," you might say, "I feel unheard when I sense that my opinions are being dismissed."

9.3 Focusing on Personal Experience

The core of an "I" statement is to express your own personal experience. By sharing your thoughts and feelings, you invite the other person to understand your perspective rather than engaging in a defensive response.

9.4 Avoiding Accusations and Blame

One of the main advantages of "I" statements is their ability to avoid assigning blame. This reduces defensiveness and encourages open dialogue, as the focus shifts from blaming to understanding.

9.5 Sharing Needs and Desires

"I" statements also allow you to communicate your needs and desires without demanding or criticizing. This approach is more likely to evoke a positive response and a willingness to work toward a resolution.

9.6 Providing Specific Examples

When using "I" statements, it can be helpful to provide specific examples to illustrate your point. This clarifies your perspective and helps the listener better grasp the situation.

9.7 Active Listening in Response

Using "I" statements often leads to more effective communication, encouraging the listener to respond with empathy and active listening. This promotes a more productive exchange of ideas and facilitates conflict resolution.

9.8 Encouraging Open Dialogue

By expressing yourself through "I" statements, you create an environment where both parties can engage in open dialogue without fear of blame or judgment. This contributes to a respectful and constructive conflict resolution process.

9.9 Chapter Summary

In this chapter, we explored the effectiveness of using "I" statements in conflict communication. By expressing your feelings, thoughts, and needs without assigning blame, you promote open dialogue, empathy, and understanding. "I" statements create an atmosphere where conflicts can be addressed constructively, ultimately leading to improved relationships and more positive outcomes.

10

Strategies for De-escalation

In this chapter, we'll delve into essential techniques for de-escalating tense situations during conflicts. We'll explore strategies that help diffuse strong emotions, promote rational thinking, and create a space for productive communication.

10.1 The Importance of De-escalation

De-escalation is the process of reducing the intensity of a conflict or tense situation. It's a crucial skill that allows individuals to regain control over their emotions and create an environment conducive to resolving conflicts constructively.

10.2 Taking Breaks

When emotions are running high, taking a break can be incredibly beneficial. Stepping away from the situation gives you time to cool off, collect your thoughts, and approach the conflict with a clearer mind.

10.3 Deep Breathing

Deep breathing is a simple yet effective technique for calming the body and mind. By taking slow, deep breaths, you activate the body's relaxation response, reducing stress and anxiety associated with conflicts.

10.4 Shifting Perspectives

Shifting your perspective involves looking at the conflict from a different angle. This can help you see the situation more objectively and consider alternative viewpoints, leading to a more balanced response.

10.5 Using Time-Outs

Time-outs are brief breaks taken during conflicts to prevent escalation. Communicate the need for a time-out respectfully, and use the time to regroup emotionally before continuing the discussion.

10.6 Practicing Mindfulness

Mindfulness involves being fully present in the moment without judgment. Practicing mindfulness during conflicts helps you stay grounded, manage emotions, and prevent impulsive reactions.

10.7 Redirecting Focus

When tensions rise, redirecting the focus of the conversation to a more neutral or positive topic can help de-escalate the situation. This shift allows everyone involved to cool down and approach the conflict with a fresh perspective.

10.8 Using Humor

Appropriately timed humor can diffuse tension and lighten the mood. Using humor shows that you're open to finding common ground and can create a more relaxed atmosphere for conflict resolution.

10.9 Seeking Commonalities

Identifying shared interests or goals can help reduce conflict intensity. Focusing on what you have in common shifts the focus away from differences, allowing for more productive conversations.

10.10 Chapter Summary

In this chapter, we explored strategies for de-escalating tense situations during conflicts. Taking breaks, practicing deep breathing, shifting perspectives, and using time-outs are techniques that help manage emotions and promote rational thinking. By incorporating these strategies, you can create an environment that fosters productive communication, ultimately leading to more effective conflict resolution.

As we conclude our exploration, remember that conflict resolution is a skill that can be honed over time. By utilizing the techniques and insights from this book, you can navigate conflicts with grace, respect, and a commitment to understanding, strengthening relationships and fostering personal growth in the process.

11

Seeking Solutions Together

In this chapter, we'll delve into the importance of seeking solutions and resolutions as a shared goal during conflicts. We'll explore the benefits of approaching conflicts as opportunities for collaborative problem-solving, leading to more positive outcomes and strengthened relationships.

11.1 The Quest for Solutions

At the heart of conflict resolution lies the goal of finding solutions that satisfy the needs and interests of all parties involved. Shifting the focus from "winning" the argument to finding common ground promotes a more constructive approach to conflicts.

11.2 Conflict as an Opportunity

Viewing conflicts as opportunities for problem-solving can transform how we approach disagreements. Instead of avoiding conflicts, we can embrace them as chances to collaborate and improve relationships.

11.3 The Value of Team Problem-Solving

Approaching conflicts as a team allows for diverse viewpoints and collective brainstorming. By working together to find solutions, conflicts become less adversarial and more collaborative.

11.4 Shared Responsibility

When both parties take responsibility for finding solutions, the burden of resolving conflicts is shared. This promotes a sense of equality and fosters an atmosphere of mutual respect.

11.5 Generating Win-Win Outcomes

Team problem-solving emphasizes the creation of win-win outcomes. This means seeking solutions that address the interests and needs of both parties, resulting in resolutions that are satisfactory to all involved.

11.6 Fostering Trust and Collaboration

Collaborative conflict resolution builds trust between parties. When individuals work together to find solutions, it creates a sense of unity and mutual understanding that can extend beyond the immediate conflict.

11.7 Encouraging Open Communication

Team problem-solving encourages open communication and active listening. Both parties are more likely to share their thoughts and concerns when they feel that their perspectives are valued and respected.

11.8 Embracing Creativity

Collaborative conflict resolution often leads to innovative solutions. By combining different ideas and viewpoints, parties can arrive at outcomes that might not have been considered individually.

11.9 Acknowledging Shared Goals

Identifying shared goals, even amid differing opinions, reinforces the idea that both parties have a common interest in resolving the conflict. This shared purpose becomes the foundation for finding solutions together.

11.10 Chapter Summary

In this chapter, we explored the importance of seeking solutions and resolutions as a shared goal during conflicts. Viewing conflicts as opportunities for collaborative problem-solving fosters trust, open communication, and creativity. By embracing team problem-solving, conflicts can be transformed into avenues for growth, understanding, and the strengthening of relationships.

As you apply these principles in your own conflict resolution journey, remember that seeking solutions together not only leads to more positive outcomes but also contributes to a culture of mutual respect and effective communication in all areas of your life.

12

Growing Through Conflict

In this final chapter, we'll reflect on the role of conflicts in relationship growth and summarize the key takeaways from this book. We'll offer guidance on how to apply the conflict resolution skills you've learned to foster personal development and improved relationships.

12.1 The Role of Conflicts in Growth

Contrary to common perception, conflicts are not solely barriers to relationships; they can be catalysts for growth. When approached with the right mindset and skills, conflicts provide opportunities for self-awareness, improved communication, and stronger connections.

12.2 Learning from Challenges

Challenges and conflicts push us beyond our comfort zones, encouraging personal development. By embracing these opportunities, we become more adaptable, resilient, and empathetic individuals.

12.3 Strengthening Relationships

Effective conflict resolution strengthens relationships by fostering open communication, mutual respect, and collaboration. When conflicts are navigated constructively, relationships emerge stronger and more resilient.

12.4 Key Takeaways

Let's recap the key takeaways from this book:

1. Respectful Communication: Mutual respect is the foundation of constructive conflict resolution. Communicate openly, without assigning blame.

2. Embrace Different Perspectives: Diverse viewpoints enrich conflict resolution. Empathetic listening and seeking understanding create a culture of collaboration.

3. Manage Emotions: Emotional awareness and regulation are vital during conflicts. Techniques like deep breathing and mindfulness help you stay composed.

4. Identify Triggers and Patterns: Recognize your triggers and patterns to break unproductive cycles and respond thoughtfully.

5. Find Common Ground: Seek shared goals and win-win solutions. Collaborative problem-solving promotes growth and understanding.

12.5 Applying Conflict Resolution Skills

To apply these skills effectively:

1. Practice Active Listening: Truly hear the other person's perspective before responding.

2. Use "I" Statements: Express your emotions and needs without assigning

blame.

3. Manage Emotions: Use de-escalation techniques like deep breathing and taking breaks.

4. Seek Solutions Together: Approach conflicts as opportunities for collaborative problem-solving.

5. Reflect and Learn: After conflicts, reflect on what you've learned about yourself and others.

12.6 Transforming Conflicts into Growth

As you apply these skills, remember that conflicts are not roadblocks, but stepping stones to personal growth and enriched relationships. Embrace the chance to navigate conflicts constructively, and you'll find that each challenge becomes an opportunity for positive transformation.

Thank you for joining us on this journey to explore the art of navigating conflicts. By fostering respect, communication, and understanding, you have the tools to transform conflicts into opportunities for growth and connection in all areas of your life.

Conclusion: Navigating Conflicts with Respect and Understanding

In a world filled with diverse perspectives and individual experiences, conflicts are an inevitable part of our interactions. However, as we've explored in this book, conflicts are not merely sources of discord; they hold the potential to be profound opportunities for growth, connection, and understanding. The journey through these chapters has illuminated the importance of respectful disagreements and effective conflict resolution in building strong, resilient relationships.

Respectful Disagreements: The Foundation of Strong Relationships

Throughout our exploration, we've emphasized the significance of mutual respect in conflict resolution. Respect creates an environment where open communication flourishes, where diverse viewpoints are celebrated, and where empathy is nurtured. By listening actively, expressing ourselves with "I" statements, and managing our emotions, we lay the groundwork for addressing conflicts in a manner that values the individuals involved and seeks to bridge differences rather than exacerbate them.

Conflicts as Opportunities for Connection

Conflicts provide us with unique opportunities to connect on a deeper level. When we approach disagreements with an open heart and a genuine desire to understand, we show that our relationships are more important than being "right." Viewing conflicts as chances to collaborate, find common ground, and generate win-win solutions transforms these moments from obstacles to stepping stones on the path to stronger connections.

Embracing the Journey

As we conclude this exploration of conflict resolution, remember that every interaction is an opportunity to apply the principles you've learned. Each conflict holds the potential to foster understanding, promote empathy, and enrich your relationships. By navigating conflicts with respect, communication, and a commitment to finding common ground, you're not only cultivating healthier connections but also contributing to a more harmonious world.

A Call to Action

In your journey ahead, embrace conflicts as opportunities for growth and connection. Approach them with an open mind and a willingness to seek understanding. Remember that the skills you've acquired—respectful communication, empathetic listening, emotional regulation, and collaborative problem-solving—are valuable tools that can guide you through the complexities of disagreements.

Thank You

Thank you for joining us on this exploration of conflict resolution. By striving to understand, communicate, and connect, you are contributing to a world where conflicts are not barriers but bridges, leading to deeper relationships and a more harmonious society. May your journey be filled with meaningful connections, personal growth, and the transformative power of respectful disagreements.

www.ingramcontent.com/pod-product-compliance
Lightning Source LLC
LaVergne TN
LVHW020456080526
838202LV00057B/5979